A Tool for The Journey—Now Faith!

A great read in every sense of the word. The author takes you on his journey of faith leaving you with a profound understanding of your own. Leveraging pastoral knowledge, he seamlessly weaves his personal views and experience with tenets from the scripture fashioning a beautiful tapestry of faith.

Written in an explanation and example format, this body of work makes for an easy and enjoyable read. Regardless of where you are currently on your spiritual journey, it provides you with the tool to gain a profound understanding of faith and how God's promises can empower you in life.

The instructional value of this body of the work cannot be understated. While the author freely takes advantage of artistic license oft moving from personal to instructional to pastoral, the theological tenets are unquestionable.

Throughout my journey to discover Christ and how the power of faith brings you closer to Him I have read several books on the subject. Until now, *Mountain Moving Faith* by Kenneth Hagen's has been my favorite. I found the instructional format of this book and the author's uses of both personal and spiritual examples throughout, have provided me with a set of valuable tools to move forward in faith.

This body of work has exceeded my expectations. It offers a hand-in-hand guide on how to elevate your spiritual walk-in-faith.

— Lisa Glaspie

A TOOL
for the
JOURNEY

DR. JEVON TURNER, SR.

NOW FAITH

A TOOL
for the
JOURNEY

Charleston, SC
www.PalmettoPublishing.com

A Tool for the Journey: Now Faith

First Edition

Hardcover ISBN: 979-8-8229-2366-9
Paperback ISBN: 979-8-8229-2367-6

Dedication

I express my deepest gratitude to my Lord and Savior, Jesus Christ, whose guidance through the Holy Spirit has made this book possible.

First and foremost, I dedicate this book to my beloved wife, Suzanne Turner. Her unwavering faithfulness during my incarceration and constant support has been the bedrock of my inspiration. She is a true reflection of God's love.

I am also grateful for my church family, The Gathering Place Worship Center, whom I am honored to serve as their pastor. Your love, encouragement, and unwavering support for my wife and me have inspired me tremendously. It is a privilege to serve you all under the direction and leadership of our Lord and Savior, Jesus Christ.

To my two sons, Jevon D. Turner Jr. and Devontè Crook, I dedicate this book with immense love and appreciation for your constant love and support. Jevon, for your service in the United States Marine Corps, and Devontè, for accepting your calling into God's ministry at the tender age of fifteen and for your remarkable talent as a Gospel rapper known as "DCrook."

I extend my heartfelt dedication to my late pastor, Richard L. Hamlett, who imparted invaluable wisdom and teachings during my journey in ministry. I am also grateful to my new pastor, Earnest Williams of Mount Zion M. B. Church, who has been a true friend and unwavering supporter. Pastor Williams, your steadfastness and guidance has meant the world to me, especially during challenging times when others turned away. Thank you for your unwavering presence!

This book is dedicated to the loving memory of my dear mother, Ethel Mae Gardner. I hold you close to my heart and will forever cherish our love. I would also like to dedicate this book to my brothers and sisters whom I discovered after forty-eight years: Rod, Todd, James, Dawn, Lynn, Leigh, and Beth.

Lastly, I want to honor the memories of two individuals who held a special place in my heart and have now departed to be with the Lord: my beloved sister, Latrece Turner, and my dear cousin, Shawn Miller. May this book inspire all who read it, just as you both inspired me.

With deep appreciation and the hope to inspire others, I offer this dedication to my loved ones and all those who have touched my life.

Table of Contents

Disclaimer

This book is intended to provide insights and reflections on the subject of faith based on the Christian perspective and the belief in God's Word. It is important to note that the views expressed in this book are those of the author and do not necessarily represent the opinions or beliefs of all individuals or religious traditions.

The content presented in this book is for informational and inspirational purposes only. It should be considered something other than professional advice or a substitute for seeking guidance from qualified religious leaders, counselors, or experts. Readers should consult with appropriate professionals regarding their specific circumstances and questions.

While every effort has been made to ensure the accuracy and reliability of the information provided in this book, the author and publisher assume no responsibility for errors, omissions, or any consequences arising from using the information herein. Furthermore, the examples and stories shared in this book are intended to illustrate principles of faith and should not be taken as literal accounts or guarantees of specific outcomes.

Individual faith experiences may vary, and readers are encouraged to interpret and apply the concepts discussed in this book according to their beliefs and convictions. The journey of faith is deeply personal, and what may work for one person may not necessarily work for another.

Finally, it is important to approach the exploration of faith with an open mind and respect for diverse perspectives. This book aims to inspire and encourage readers on their faith journeys, but it is not intended to impose or invalidate any individual's beliefs or religious practices.

By reading this book, you acknowledge and agree to the above disclaimer. The author and publisher disclaim any liability or responsibility for any loss or damage incurred as a direct or indirect result of using or applying the information presented in this book.

Introduction

In a world often characterized by uncertainty and doubt, there is a powerful force that has the potential to ignite our spirits, guide our steps, and transform our lives. That force is faith. Faith is not merely a passive belief or a fleeting hope; it is a steadfast conviction in something greater than ourselves. For countless individuals throughout history, faith has been anchored in the Word of God.

In this journey of exploration, we delve into the essence of faith and its profound connection to God's Word. We will uncover the remarkable stories of men and women who exemplified unwavering faith in the face of adversity, drawing inspiration from their experiences. From their stories, we will learn how to accept the call for faith in our own lives, overcome doubt and uncertainty, and surrender to the divine plan and will.

However, the road of faith is not without challenges. We will encounter moments that test the very fabric of our convictions, and trials that threaten to dim the flame of faith within us. Yet we will discover the power to persevere, to overcome obstacles, and to activate "Now Faith" in the midst of our challenges.

As Christians, faith is not confined to mere belief; it is a way of life. We will explore how to apply "Now Faith" in practical ways, living in obedience to God's commands, trusting in His promises, and stepping out in faith to take action. Moreover, as leaders, we will learn how to inspire others, make decisions rooted in faith rather than fear, and empower those around us to walk boldly in their own journeys of faith.

In this exploration, we will come to understand that having "Now Faith" doesn't always change our direction; instead, it allows us to navigate life's storms with unwavering trust in God's sovereignty. We will find peace and contentment in knowing that His plan surpasses our understanding and that His wisdom and guidance are far greater than our own expectations.

Through the storms we face, we will realize that God has chosen us for a purpose. In the midst of difficult seasons, we will grow spiritually, gaining wisdom, strength, and resilience. And as we journey forward, we will find ourselves equipped to encourage others, sharing the lessons we have learned along the way.

Above all, we will discover that true faith lies not in our own abilities, but in trusting in the character and faithfulness of God. We will learn to let go of self-reliance, surrendering our lives to His will, and recognizing that it is in His hands that our faith finds its greatest strength.

So let us embark on this transformative journey together, embracing faith as our unwavering guide, our source of strength, and our newfound tool for navigating the challenges of life. As we explore the remarkable power of faith, may our hearts be captivated, our spirits engaged, and our lives forever transformed.

Unveiling the Power of God's Word in Believers' Faith

As I began writing this book, I found myself confronted with numerous questions about faith. What exactly is faith? Why is it necessary in our lives? What can faith accomplish for us? Why does it hold such immense significance? I realized I needed to delve deeper into the true essence of faith, for our relationship with God can only truly begin when we possess unwavering faith in Him. Through our faith in God, we come to recognize our deliverance from the burdens of our past, achieved through the sacrificial death of Christ on the cross.

Despite my years of attending church and delivering countless sermons, I never anticipated that the day would come when my faith would be put to the ultimate test. The time I spent in incarceration compelled me to seek a profound understanding of the genuine meaning of faith. During that dark period, I knew my faith would be questioned if I didn't strive to comprehend how God responds to our unwavering trust in Him.

I genuinely believe that if every person claiming to be a Christian were completely honest with themselves and God, they would all admit that there have been moments in their lives when their faith has been tested to such an extent that they've questioned their comprehension of it.

There have been instances where their faith has been tested to the point of wondering if God is truly present. Understanding faith is crucial for the foundation of our relationship with God. Without a tested and steadfast faith, I believe we cannot truly grasp the essence of God and His reactions when we wholeheartedly trust Him.

When I examined the word "faith," the initial two words of the first verse in the eleventh chapter of Hebrews stood out with resounding clarity: "Now Faith"! These two words captured my attention so profoundly that it felt as if my soul had suddenly slammed on the brakes. I experienced a sensation like running a stop sign at a treacherous intersection. I noticed these two words in a way I had never done before. Perhaps it was because my faith was teetering on the edge of the most significant trial of my life. Nevertheless, without these two words, I would have been destined for a head-on collision at the crossroads of life.

The word "now" signifies the present moment, the current state in which we find ourselves. On the other hand, "faith" encompasses belief and unwavering confidence. As followers of Christ, we must possess "Now Faith"! We must firmly believe and be confident that God can handle any situation we encounter. During your current life circumstances, you might be weathering a ferocious storm. However, rest assured that God can and will guide you through, even when it seems as though He is distant or unresponsive. Remember, He is always closer than you realize.

God is omnipresent, meaning He is ever present everywhere and at every moment. His unchanging nature guarantees His steadfastness!

As Christians, we must cultivate what I refer to as "patient endurance." A profound connection exists between faith and patient endurance. **Hebrews 11:1** is intimately linked to **verses 38–39** of the preceding chapter, where we are explicitly urged to endure during persecution. We must remain resolute in our faith in God, refusing to waver. By demonstrating patient endurance, we validate the authenticity of our faith. Faith looks forward to an anticipated and hoped-for future. Patient endurance is necessitated because this future is replete with yet unrealized hopes.

Living by faith necessitates our ability to endure patiently. From my experience of incarceration, I have learned that God desires us to be patient. We must comprehend that God's timetable does not align with our own. My grandmother used to say, "He may not arrive when you want Him to, but He is always punctual."

God will execute His perfect plan for us at the most opportune moment. The most profound revelation of the significance of patient endurance occurred during the darkest hour of my life: when my wife drove me to jail to surrender myself after all my appeals had been exhausted. I will never forget when my wife parked the car, her eyes filled with tears as she gazed at me with profound sadness. In that heart-wrenching instant, she asked, "Darling, shall I drive away and we run off together? I know you are innocent, as I observed every piece of evidence, and none implicated you. So if you wish, we can escape this ordeal."

Despite my weakened faith and the sense that God was absent, I responded swiftly and firmly, "My love, I must tread this path, for there is a lesson God desires me to learn."

Patient endurance is not attained effortlessly or without cost. As I turned away from the car, I refrained from looking back because my heart was overwhelmed with sorrow, and my faith was shaken. In my moment of utmost vulnerability, I could hear the Holy Spirit ministering to my soul through **Psalm 27:14**, which implores us to

> **[W]ait on the Lord: be of good courage, and He shall
> strengthen thine heart: wait, I say, on the Lord. (KJV)
> Let us hold fast the profession of our faith without wavering;
> (for He is faithful that promised). (Hebrews 10:23, KJV)
> Now faith is the substance of things hoped for, the evidence
> of things not seen. (Hebrews 11:1, KJV)**

Confidence and certainty are two defining qualities of the Christian faith that require a solid foundation. The beginning point of faith lies in believing in the unwavering character of God. He is exactly who He claims to be. The endpoint is trusting God's promise; he will fulfill what He has spoken. Even when we don't see these promises materializing, our unwavering belief in God's faith demonstrates a true, persistent faith.

In the Gospel of John, Jesus tells Thomas that those who believe without seeing are blessed. As Christians, we face the challenge of believing in something intangible. However, our faith in Jesus Christ is of utmost importance and significance. When life presents us with overwhelming situations, often leaving us feeling lost and uncertain, the solution lies in placing our complete trust in Jesus Christ.

When I entered prison, I found myself relating to the disciple Thomas. Like Thomas, I knew of Jesus's resurrection and believed in His truthful teachings. Having spent considerable time with Jesus as one of His twelve disciples, Thomas witnessed extraordinary events such as the miraculous feeding of the five thousand and His prophecies of death and resurrection. Given this firsthand knowledge, one would expect Thomas to possess unwavering faith in the disciples' accounts of Jesus's resurrection. However, Thomas doubted and insisted on seeing Jesus with his own eyes.

Similarly, God called me to preach at twelve, echoing Thomas's doubts and desires for personal confirmation. Despite accepting Christ at the age of nine and experiencing His presence and divine interventions both in my life and the lives of others, my journey mirrored Thomas's struggle. As a young child standing before a congregation, I could feel God's presence while delivering sermons. During that time, I recalled a prayer I fervently uttered upon embracing my ministry's calling—to become more Christlike each day of my life. I longed to encounter experiences akin to those endured by Jesus, thus ensuring that I would never lose sight of the profound significance of God the Father, God the Son, and God the Holy Spirit.

In essence—like Thomas—I, too, share a profound understanding and connection with the teachings of Jesus. Through personal encounters, I have witnessed His transformative power and have been granted the privilege of serving Him as a preacher.

However, Thomas, a member of the Twelve by the name of Didymus, was not present when Jesus arrived. Therefore, the other disciples told him that we had seen the Lord. But he said to them, "I will not believe unless I see the print of the nails in his hands, put my finger into the print of the nails, and thrust my hand into his side." And after eight days, his disciples returned, together with Thomas: then Jesus entered, locked the doors, stood in the center, and said, peace be unto you. Then he instructs Thomas, "Reach your finger here and see my hands; reach your hands here and press them into my side; and do not be unbelieving but believing." Thomas responded by addressing him as "my Lord and my God." Jesus said unto him, "Thomas, because thou has seen me, thou has believed: blessed are they that have not seen, and yet have believed." (John 20:24–29, KJV)

In our daily lives, we often face situations where the outcome seems uncertain, whether major challenges or minor setbacks. We must hold steadfast to our faith in Jesus Christ during these times, trusting that He will guide us through. I recall a particularly daunting experience when I stood before a judge and jury, falsely accused of a crime. The prospects appeared grim as I was confronted with the possibility of three ten-year sentences in state prison. Yet, during this dire situation, I knew I needed to place my unwavering faith in God, knowing He would be by my side no matter what. While I struggled to comprehend why everything seemed to be going wrong, I remained steadfast in my trust that God would lead me out of this challenging ordeal.

As I confronted this darkness, this seemingly impossible mountain and this profound valley of despair, as I began enduring the relentless storm, I had to activate my "Now Faith." Despite everything going awry, my so-called friends abandoning me, some members of my Christian family turning their backs, and even old friends turning against me, I had to dig deep within myself and allow my spiritual strength to rise. Wherever you may find yourself in life, I encourage you to let your inner spirit soar and activate your own "Now Faith."

I distinctly remember my wife urging me to maintain my faith in God, recounting the remarkable things she had witnessed Him accomplish. Yet I found myself wrestling with doubt, much like the disciple Thomas. I yearned to witness a miracle from Jesus for myself. Looking back, I realize I should have had more faith. At that point in my life, I had been a Christian for two decades and had preached for seventeen years. I had witnessed God performing countless miracles in the lives of others. He had guided me through numerous trials before, but doubt had crept into my heart for some inexplicable reason. Indeed, doubt often infiltrates our faith when it is tested from all sides. Nevertheless, we must remember that relief lies in recognizing that our Shepherd is truly our guide. The strength of our faith depends on our connection to His Word.

It was not until my first day in prison that my faith was restored to its rightful place. Just as Jesus had spoken to doubting Thomas, He spoke to me. I will always remember His words: "Come here, Jevon. Do not rely on your understanding. Place your hand in mine and never let go. I will carry you through this trial in your life. I will never abandon or forsake you. Put your complete trust in me. I called you to preach My Word from the moment you were formed in your mother's womb. I want you to proclaim My message every season, no matter the circumstances. Your trial will be immense, but endure it, for it will become a testament to the world in due time."

When the divine presence of the Lord departed from me, a captivating sight caught my attention: a resplendent robin was perched upon the window ledge just above my confinement. The bird delicately held a strand of straw entwined with a worm in its beak. Illuminated by a radiant light, the scene evoked a profound sense of awe and stirred the voice of the Lord within my soul once again. His Words resonated deeply as He spoke to me, conveying a profound message: "The worm symbolizes that I shall sustain you with My Word throughout this arduous trial, and the straw signifies that once I have nourished you, I will guide you to solid ground." Inexpressible joy and an unwavering faith surged within me. How truly magnificent is the God we serve!

The Lord directed me to three scriptural passages, the first being **Revelations 12:11: "And they overcame him by the blood of the Lamb and by the word of their testimony; and they loved not their lives unto the death." (KJV)**

When Jesus Christ, through His sacrificial death, shed His blood for the expiation of our sins, Satan was decisively defeated. The triumph was achieved through Christ's selfless act on the cross, where He bore the punishment for our transgressions. We can confront adversity by placing our unwavering faith in Him. Rather than succumbing to fear or attempting to evade hardship, we should remain steadfast in our devotion to Christ, acknowledging the magnitude of His sacrifice and the victory He bestows upon us.

The second Scripture the Lord led me to was **Romans 8:31–39:**

What shall we then say to these things? If God be for us, who can be against us? He that spared not his own Son, but delivered him up for us all, how shall he not with him also freely give us all things? Who shall lay anything to the charge of God's elect? It is God that justifieth. Who is he that condemneth? It is Christ that died, yea rather, that is risen again, who is even at the right hand of God, who also maketh intercession for us. Who shall separate us from the love of Christ? shall tribulation, or distress, or persecution, or famine, or nakedness, or peril, or sword? As it is written, for thy sake we are killed all the day long; we are accounted as sheep for the slaughter. Nay, in all these things we are more than conquerors through him that loved us. For I am persuaded, that neither death, nor life, nor angels, nor principalities, nor powers, nor things present, nor things to come, Nor height, nor depth, nor any other creature, shall be able to separate us from the love of God, which is in Christ Jesus our Lord. (KJV)

Regardless of our circumstances or location, we can never be separated from God's love. Instead of driving us away from Him, suffering can deepen our identification with Him and allow His love to reach and heal us. During testing, we must learn to activate our "Now Faith" and hold onto the promises found in God's Word, which strengthen our faith.

It is crucial to recognize that nothing can hinder God's constant presence with us. He is omnipresent, always with us, even in the darkest moments. As the Psalmist David said, **"If I make my bed in hell, behold, [God is] there." (Psalm 139:8, KJV)** Reflecting on this, I chuckled at the thought that being in prison felt close to being in hell, but even in that situation, God was there when no one else was. God assures us of His immense love to instill complete security in Him. If we truly believe in these overwhelming assurances, we will face anything without fear as our faith stands strong in adversity.

The third Scripture that came to mind was **Romans 8:28: "And we know that all things work together for good to them that love God, to them who are the called according to his purpose." (KJV)** God orchestrates everything for our ultimate good, even when the situation appears bleak. Although this doesn't mean that everything that happens to us will be pleasant, God, in His sovereignty, can turn things around for our long-term benefit. It is essential to remember that God's purpose is not solely to make us happy but to fulfill His purpose in our lives. We were created not for our glory but for the glory of God. This verse's promise applies only to those who love God and align themselves with His plans. You must ask yourself, "Am I fitting into God's plan?" The called are those whom the Holy Spirit convinces and enables to receive Christ for the purpose He has for them. When we embrace God's purpose for our lives, our perspective on life shifts, our mindset changes, and we begin to see things in a completely different light. We learn to walk by faith, not by sight. Our trust lies in God, not in earthly treasures. We seek security in Heaven, not on Earth. We learn to accept, rather than resent, pain and persecution because we know that God is with us.

In every circumstance that life presents us, placing our trust unwaveringly in God is crucial. True faith means trusting Him even when we cannot comprehend the reasons behind certain events. It requires complete confidence in God's ability to guide us through any situation.

I can attest that God will support and sustain you, even in your darkest moments. Imagine sitting in a confined six-by-nine cell with a metal sheet as your bed, barely two inches from a toilet. Night after night, the cries of weary men fill the air, making it impossible to find rest while questioning why you're there and struggling to hold onto your faith. Yet even in this profound darkness, I learned to trust God, who revealed Himself as my strength and redeemer.

At this stage of my life, my faith no longer depends on being delivered from adversity. Instead, my faith is firmly rooted in the certainty that the Lord will accompany me every step of the way. Faith means sometimes anticipating storms while seeking the rainbow as God carries us through. Our hope in Christ Jesus allows us to grasp the unseen things.

Even as I write these words and reflect on my time in prison, I have discovered the importance of firmly grasping God's unchanging hand. I understand this is merely the beginning of a journey that will test my faith. Regardless of how arduous it may appear, do not allow your circumstances to diminish your faith in God. Remember the words of **Hebrews 10:23**, which instruct us to **"hold fast to the profession of [your] faith without wavering." (KJV)** God will bring you through.

In **Luke 17:5–6**, the Bible says, **"And the apostles said unto the Lord, increase our faith. And the Lord said, if ye had faith as a grain of mustard seed, ye might say unto this sycamine tree, be thou plucked up by the root, and be thou planted in the sea: and it should obey you." (KJV)** All we require is a mustard-seed-sized amount of faith. The magnitude of our faith is inconsequential to God; what matters is the sincerity of our faith. God desires us to rely completely on Him in times of prosperity and adversity. But what does faith truly entail? It encompasses wholeheartedly relying on God and being willing to fulfill

His will. It entails complete and humble obedience to God's commands and a readiness to do whatever He calls us to do. Therefore, regardless of your challenges, always maintain your faith in an omnipotent God.

Now join me on a journey to explore the true nature of faith.

CHAPTER ONE

Understanding What Faith Is

"Now Faith" can be defined as a deep, unwavering trust and belief in God that transcends the present circumstances. It is the ability to have confidence in God's promises and guidance, even when it seems intangible or contradictory to the natural realm. "Now Faith" is based on the knowledge that God has perfect timing and that His methods are higher than ours.

As a believer in Christ, faith in God's Word is a fundamental aspect of your spiritual journey. Faith can be understood as complete trust, confidence, and belief in something or someone. In Christianity, faith refers to placing your trust and confidence in God and His Word, as revealed in the Bible.

Hebrews 11:1: "Now faith is the assurance of things hoped for, the conviction of things not seen." (ESV) This is a verse from the New Testament Bible, specifically from the Book of Hebrews. It speaks about the nature of faith, describing it as the assurance or confident expectation of things hoped for and the conviction or firm belief in things that are not evident. This verse highlights the importance of trust and belief in the Christian faith, even when we cannot physically perceive or fully understand what we hope for.

Another verse which supports understanding what faith is in God's Word is **Romans 10:17: "So faith comes from hearing, and hearing through the word of Christ." (ESV)** This is a verse from the Book of Romans in the New Testament. It emphasizes that faith is obtained through hearing, particularly through the proclamation and teaching of the Word of Christ. This verse suggests that hearing Christ's message, the Bible's teachings, and believers' testimony can generate faith within individuals.

Genuine faith believes in what Christ has done for us. It's in the Bible. **Romans 5:1: "Therefore, having been justified by faith, we have peace with God through our Lord Jesus Christ." (NKJV)**

Faith is trusting God all the time. It's in the Bible. **Hebrews 10:38: "Now the just shall live by faith: but if any man draw back, my soul shall have no pleasure in him." (KJV)**

Weak faith can become strong with God's help. It's in the Bible. **Mark 9:24: "And straightway the father of the child cried out, and said with tears, Lord, I believe; help thou mine unbelief." (KJV)**

Faith is a deep trust and confidence in God, His character, and His promises. It involves wholeheartedly relying on Him and believing He is faithful and trustworthy. Faith is a firm belief in the unseen and spiritual realities. It goes beyond what can be perceived by our physical senses and embraces the truth of God's existence, His nature, and His work in the world.

Faith is an assurance and hope in things not yet realized. It involves a confident expectation that God will fulfill His promises and accomplish His purposes, even when circumstances may appear contrary. Faith is an essential component of a relationship with God. It plays a central role in salvation; individuals are justified before God and receive His grace through faith. It also enables believers to fellowship with Him, experience His presence, and grow spiritually. Faith encompasses trust, belief, assurance, hope, and active response, all centered on a personal relationship with God. It is a foundational element of the Christian life and a vital aspect of experiencing God's love, guidance, and transformation.

The Role of God's Word in Faith

The Word of God, as revealed in the Bible, plays a crucial role in the development and expression of faith according to the Bible. Here are a few key aspects of the Word of God concerning faith:

1. Revelation of God's Character and Promises

The Bible is God's inspired Word, providing a comprehensive revelation of His character, nature, and redemptive plan for humanity. Through Scripture, we know who God is, His faithfulness, and His promises. The Word of God gives us a foundation for our faith by showing us God's attributes and His track record of fulfilling His promises.

2. Source of Faith

Romans 10:17 states, **"So faith comes from hearing, and hearing through the word of Christ." (ESV)** The Word of God is instrumental in generating and increasing faith. As we engage with the Scriptures through reading, hearing, or studying, we encounter the truths and testimonies that inspire and strengthen our faith.

3. Guidance and Direction

Psalm 119:105 says, **"Your word is a lamp to my feet and a light to my path." (ESV)** The Word of God provides guidance, wisdom, and clarity for our lives. It illuminates our path, helping us make decisions, discern God's will, and navigate challenges. It reveals God's principles and instructions, shaping our understanding of living according to His purposes.

4. Nourishment and Spiritual Growth

Just as physical nourishment is vital for our bodies, the Word of God is essential for our spiritual growth. **1 Peter 2:2** says, **"Like newborn**

infants, long for the pure spiritual milk, that by it you may grow up into salvation." (ESV) Regularly immersing ourselves in God's Word enables us to grow in knowledge, wisdom, and maturity in our faith.

5. Weapon Against Doubt and Temptation

When faced with doubts, temptations, or spiritual warfare, Jesus Himself demonstrated the power of the Word of God as a defense. In **Matthew 4:4,** Jesus said, **"Man shall not live by bread alone, but by every word that comes from the mouth of God." (ESV)** By knowing and applying God's Word, we are equipped to resist the lies and schemes of the enemy and remain steadfast in our faith.

CHAPTER TWO

Biblical Examples of Faith in God's Word

Faith is an essential aspect of Christianity and is defined as complete trust in something or someone. In Christianity, faith refers to believing in God and accepting His Word, as revealed in the Bible. The Bible inspires faith and provides examples of people who had great faith in God.

The importance of faith in Christianity cannot be overstated. Faith is the foundation on which the believer's relationship with God is built and is essential for the Christian's spiritual growth and development. In **Hebrews 11:6**, the Bible says, **"But without faith it is impossible to please him: for he that cometh to God must believe that he is, and that he is a rewarder of them that diligently seek him." (KJV)** This verse emphasizes faith's crucial role in the Christian's relationship with God.

I will speak on five people from the Bible who exemplified great faith in God. These examples serve as a source of inspiration and encouragement and demonstrate the power of faith to shape the lives of believers. Readers will obtain a better grasp of the value of faith and its role in the lives of Christians by studying the lives of these biblical figures.

Five People from the Bible Who Exemplified Great Faith in God
1. Abraham's Faith

Abraham is one of the most prominent figures in the Bible and is often called the Father of Faith. Abraham's background is rooted in the Book of Genesis, where he is described as a man of great faith and obedience to God. Abraham's faith was tested when God called him to leave his homeland and venture to a place God would show him. Despite his lack of clarity about God's plan, Abraham obeyed God's call and set out on his journey.

Abraham's obedience to God's call is a powerful example of his unwavering faith in God. Abraham's faith was not based on his understanding, but on his trust in God's plan for his life. This obedience demonstrated Abraham's faith in God's promises and laid the foundation for his relationship with God. In **Genesis 15:6**, the Bible says, **"And he believed in the Lord; and he counted it to him for righteousness."** **(KJV)** This verse highlights the significance of Abraham's faith in the Bible and how it was counted as righteousness in the eyes of God.

Abraham's faith is still remembered and celebrated today as an example of what it means to have great faith in God. It serves as a reminder that faith is not just a concept, but a way of life.

Through his obedience to God's call, Abraham demonstrated the power of faith to shape a person's life and direct his path. By studying Abraham's faith, readers can be inspired to cultivate a similar level of trust and obedience in their relationship with God.

2. Moses's Faith

Moses is another prominent figure in the Bible, and he is known for his unwavering faith in God. Moses's background is rooted in the Book of Exodus, where he is depicted as a leader of the Israelites who God called to lead his people out of slavery in Egypt. Moses initially hesitated to accept God's call, but ultimately trusted God's plan for his life and obeyed his command.

Moses's trust in God's plan is a powerful example of his faith in God. Despite several hurdles and problems, Moses maintained his faith in God and depended on his guidance throughout his journey. This act of trust demonstrated Moses's faith in God's power and wisdom and served as an example of how faith can shape a person's life. In **Deuteronomy 31:8**, the Bible says, **"And the Lord, He is the one who goes before you. He will be with you, He will not leave you nor forsake you; do not fear nor be dismayed." (NKJV)** This verse highlights the significance of Moses's faith in the Bible and how God's presence and guidance sustained him on his journey.

The faith of Moses is still remembered and celebrated today as an example of what it means to have great faith in God. It serves as a reminder that faith is not just a concept, but a way of life.

Through his trust in God's plan, Moses demonstrated the power of faith to direct a person's path and guide him through difficult circumstances. By studying the faith of Moses, readers can be inspired to cultivate a similar level of trust in God and his guidance in their own lives.

3. Job's Faith

Job is another example of a person of great faith in the Bible. He is best known for his unwavering belief in the goodness of God despite suffering numerous trials and hardships. The Book of Job provides background on Job as a wealthy man who lived a righteous life but was suddenly struck by numerous misfortunes and personal loss. Despite these difficulties, Job maintained faith in God and trusted his goodness.

Job's unwavering belief in the goodness of God is a testament to the strength of his faith. Despite facing extreme hardships and questioning the reasons for his suffering, Job refused to turn away from God and continued to trust in His character. In **Job 13:15**, Job says, **"Though he slay me, yet will I trust in him: but I will maintain mine own ways before him." (KJV)** This verse highlights the depth of Job's faith and his unwavering belief in God, even in adversity.

Job's faith in God has significant implications for Christians today. By studying the story of Job, readers can be inspired to cultivate a similar level of trust in God, even when faced with difficult circumstances. Job's example also serves as a reminder that faith is not just about feeling good or experiencing positive results, but rather about trusting in God's goodness and character, regardless of the circumstances. Through the story of Job, readers can learn to trust in God's love, wisdom, and sovereignty over all things.

4. Mary's Faith

Mary, the mother of Jesus, is another example of great faith in the Bible. Mary's background can be found in the Gospels of Matthew and Luke, where she is depicted as a young woman who was visited by the angel Gabriel and told that she would bear God's Son. Despite this new, unexpected, and seemingly impossible nature, Mary was willing to accept God's plan for her life.

Mary's willingness to accept God's plan is a testimony to her faith. She trusted the Lord's sovereignty and recognized that His plan for her was good, even though it was not what she expected or desired. Mary's faith is also evident in her song of praise, known as the Magnificat, where she declares in **Luke 1:45: "And blessed is she that believed: for there shall be a performance of those things which were told her from the Lord." (KJV)**

The significance of Mary's faith in the Bible lies in her role as a model for Christians today. Mary's example shows that faith involves surrendering our plans and desires to God and trusting in His goodness and sovereignty. Following Mary's example, Christians can learn to trust God's plan for their lives, even when it is not what they expected or wanted. Through the story of Mary, we can be inspired to place our faith in the Lord and trust in His wisdom and love.

5. Peter's Faith

Peter, one of the twelve apostles, is another example of great faith in the Bible. Peter's background can be found throughout the gospels, where he is depicted as a fisherman called by Jesus to be a disciple. Through his time with Jesus, Peter experienced a transformation in his faith.

Peter's transformation through faith is demonstrated in his actions and words. Initially, Peter was often impulsive and lacked understanding, but as he spent time with Jesus, his faith grew, and he understood better who Jesus was and the meaning of his mission. This is seen in Peter's confession in **Matthew 16:16**, where he says, **"Thou art the Christ, the Son of the living God." (KJV)** Peter's faith continued to grow, even as he faced trials and difficulties, as evidenced by his teaching and leadership in the early church.

The significance of Peter's faith in the Bible lies in his role as a model for Christians today. Peter's story demonstrates that faith is not static but can grow and mature over time. Through Peter's transformation, we can learn that faith involves a process of continual growth and that we can grow in our understanding and trust in God by spending time with Him. Peter's example also shows us that faith can overcome our weaknesses and that, with the help of the Holy Spirit, we can become strong witnesses for Christ.

Chapter Three

Accepting the Call for Faith

The quest for meaning and purpose takes many forms in a world brimming with diverse perspectives and countless paths. Among the myriad journeys we embark upon, one beckons us with an enduring call: the journey of faith. It is a profound and transformative odyssey that reaches deep into the recesses of our souls, guiding us toward a higher understanding of ourselves, others, and the mysteries that encompass our existence.

Accepting the call for faith is an intimate and personal decision that often arises from a yearning for truth and a desire for a more profound sense of belonging. It invites us to shed the armor of skepticism and embark on a journey where doubts and uncertainties become stepping-stones to deeper insight and unwavering conviction.

This journey is not without its challenges. It demands courage, humility, and an open mind. It requires us to examine our beliefs, question our assumptions, and confront the shadows within our souls. Yet in the face of these challenges, embracing the call for faith can ignite a flame within us that illuminates our path, instills hope in times of darkness, and empowers us to navigate life's tumultuous seas with unwavering resilience.

Recognizing the Call for Faith in Your Life

As a believer, I am deeply moved by the call for faith. It is not a coincidence or a random occurrence, but a profound experience that resonates within the depths of my being. It is a call that speaks to the core of my existence and ignites a fire within my soul.

I recognize this call as a divine intervention orchestrated by the loving hand of God Himself. He has reached out to me, drawing me closer to Him, awakening my spirit to His presence. His grace humbles me, for it is by His initiative that I have been led to this path of faith.

Through prayer, reflection, and immersion in His Word, the Holy Scriptures, I have found solace and guidance. The verses within the Bible breathe life into my journey of faith, providing a steadfast foundation upon which I stand. **Romans 8:30** assures me that those whom God calls, He also justifies and glorifies, reminding me that my faith journey is part of His divine plan for my life.

> **For it is by grace you have been saved, through faith—and this is not from yourselves, it is the gift of God—not by works, so that no one can boast. (Ephesians 2:8–9, NIV)**

I am reminded that faith is indeed a gift from God. It is not something I can achieve through my own merits or efforts. Through His boundless grace, I have been saved, and through my faith, I have been granted access to this wondrous gift.

The longing for purpose and eternity, which **Ecclesiastes 3:11** speaks of, reverberates within me. I am acutely aware of the yearning in my heart, the desire for a connection with the divine. This longing has propelled me to seek God, surrender my life to Him, and embark on this journey of faith.

Above all, I recognize Jesus Christ as the embodiment of truth and the gateway to salvation. In **John 14:6,** His Words resound with unwavering certainty, proclaiming Him as the way, the truth, and the life. Through Him, I find hope, redemption, and the assurance of eternal life in the loving embrace of our Heavenly Father.

As a believer, I am eternally grateful for the call to faith in my life. It is a call that has transformed me, giving me purpose, hope, and a profound sense of belonging. I embrace this call, and with unwavering devotion, I commit myself to a lifelong journey of deepening my faith, seeking a closer relationship with God, and sharing His love with others. **Proverbs 3:5–6** reminds me to **"trust in the Lord with all [my] heart and lean not on [my] own understanding; [but to] acknowledge Him [in all my ways], and He will make [my] paths straight." (NIV)**

In the realm of faith, a journey begins, where doubt and uncertainty cast shadows upon the path. Yet, as a believer in the grace and truth of our Lord, I shall rise above the storm of uncertainty, accepting the call to embrace faith.

As believers, it is not uncommon to experience doubt and uncertainty, especially when faced with challenges or questions that seem to have limited scriptural support. However, there are ways to navigate these situations and strengthen your faith. Here are a few suggestions:

1. Seek a Deeper Understanding

While there may be limited scriptural support for a particular issue or question, exploring related principles or concepts in the Scriptures is worth exploring. Look for broader themes or teachings that shed light on the topic. Consult reputable commentaries, books, or resources that provide insights from trusted scholars or theologians.

2. Engage in Prayer and Meditation

Spend time in prayer, seeking guidance and understanding from God. Seek a personal connection with the divine and ask for clarity and peace regarding your doubts and uncertainties. Meditation can also help calm the mind and create space for spiritual insights to emerge.

3. Seek Wisdom from Trusted Mentors

Engage in discussions with wise and knowledgeable individuals within your faith community who can offer guidance and share their experiences. Their perspectives might provide new insights and points of view that can help you navigate your doubts.

4. Embrace Intellectual Exploration

Faith and reason can coexist. Engage in intellectual exploration by reading books and articles and listening to podcasts or lectures that address topics related to your doubts. Seek out religious and secular perspectives to gain a broader understanding.

5. Emphasize Personal Experience

Reflect on your own experiences with your faith. Consider moments when you felt a deep connection, peace, or guidance. Such experiences can serve as reminders of your faith's reality, even without extensive scriptural support for a specific issue.

6. Cultivate Trust and Surrender

Recognize that faith inherently involves an element of trust and surrender. Trust that there is wisdom and purpose beyond what you can fully comprehend. Surrender your doubts and uncertainties to God, allowing you to embrace the mystery and complexity of faith.

Surrendering to God's Plan and Will

Surrendering to God's plan and will is an act of faith and trust in a higher power. It involves acknowledging that God's wisdom and guidance surpass our limited understanding and willingly yielding control of our lives to His divine purpose. Accepting the call for faith and surrendering to God's plan requires a deep conviction and a willingness to let go of our desires and expectations.

Here are a few key aspects to consider when accepting the call for faith and surrendering to God's plan and will:

1. Trusting in God's Wisdom

Surrendering to God's plan means recognizing that His wisdom is greater than ours. It involves having faith that God knows what is best for us, even when we don't understand His ways or the paths He is leading us on. Trusting in His wisdom lets us release our anxieties and fears, knowing He is in control.

2. Letting Go of Control

Surrendering to God's will requires relinquishing our need for control. It means acknowledging that we are not the ultimate authorities in our lives, but that God holds the ultimate authority. Letting go of control involves humbling ourselves and acknowledging that we depend on God for guidance, provision, and purpose.

3. Prayer and Seeking God's Guidance

A prayer is a powerful tool for surrendering to God's plan. Through prayer, we communicate with God, seeking His guidance and aligning our hearts with His will. Regularly praying and meditating allows us to develop a deeper relationship with God and open ourselves up to receiving His guidance and direction.

4. Aligning Our Desires with God's Will

Surrendering to God's plan doesn't mean abandoning our desires and dreams. Rather, it involves aligning our desires with His will. Our aspirations fit with what God has intended for us as we draw closer to Him and seek His guidance. This alignment allows us to pursue our passions and dreams in a way that is in harmony with God's purpose for our lives.

5. Embracing Faith in the Face of Uncertainty

Surrendering to God's plan often requires stepping into the unknown and embracing uncertainty. It means faith in God's promises and believing He will guide us through even the most challenging circumstances. Trusting God's plan may not always make sense from a human perspective, but faith allows us to see beyond our limited understanding and rely on God's faithfulness.

CHAPTER FOUR

The Challenges After the Call of Faith

As a believer in Christ, I understand that the call of faith comes with its challenges. It is important to recognize that challenges are a natural part of our journey and should be expected. The Bible teaches us that we will face trials and tribulations. However, as believers, we have the assurance that God is with us every step of the way, providing us with strength, guidance, and comfort.

One of the challenges we may encounter after answering the call of faith is the testing of our faith. This can take various forms, such as doubt, questioning, or facing difficult circumstances that challenge our beliefs. In these moments, it is crucial to remember that faith is not based solely on feelings or circumstances but on our unwavering trust in God's promises. It is an opportunity to deepen our relationship with Him, seeking His wisdom and understanding through prayer, studying His Word, and seeking guidance from fellow believers.

The Testing of Faith

Testing of faith serves a purpose in our spiritual growth and development. Just as gold is refined through fire, our faith is refined through trials. During these times, we are given an opportunity to demonstrate the depth of our trust in God and grow in our dependence on Him.

When we face testing of faith, it can be a struggle to hold on to our beliefs and convictions. Doubts may arise, and we may question why God allows certain challenges to come our way. However, in these moments, we can lean on God even more, seeking His guidance, strength, and wisdom. As believers, we are encouraged to persevere through testing. The apostle James writes, **"Consider it pure joy, my brothers and sisters, whenever you face trials of many kinds, because you know that the testing of your faith produces perseverance. Let perseverance finish its work so that you may be mature and complete, not lacking anything."** (James 1:2–4, NIV)

Through testing, our faith can be strengthened and deepened. We can develop a greater sense of reliance on God and His promises. It is an opportunity to grow in understanding His character and experience His faithfulness firsthand.

During testing, it is essential to stay connected to God through prayer, reading His Word, and seeking the support of fellow believers. We can find encouragement and solace in the stories of those who have gone before us who faced trials and tribulations but remained faithful to God.

Persevering Through Trials

As a believer, I understand that persevering through trials is one of the challenges we face after answering the call of faith. When we decide to commit our lives to Jesus and follow Him, we go out on a path that is not always straightforward and easy. Jesus promised that we would face tribulations **(John 16:33)**.

However, as believers, we have hope and strength that sustains us through the toughest times. We know that God is with us, and He never forsakes us. He is our refuge and strength, an ever-present help in trouble **(Psalm 46:1)**. This knowledge gives us the confidence to face trials head-on, knowing that we are not alone in our struggles. Perseverance is not simply enduring trials with a grim determination; it is an active response fueled by our faith. It involves clinging to God's promises and seeking His guidance in every situation. We can find encouragement and wisdom through prayer, reading His Word, and seeking the support of fellow believers. In **James 1:12**, we are reminded that **"Blessed is the man that endureth temptation: for when he is tried, he shall receive the crown of life, which the Lord hath promised to them that love him." (KJV)**

Perseverance also means trusting in God's perfect timing and purpose. We may only sometimes understand why we face certain trials or why they last as long as they do. Still, we can trust that God is working all things together for our good **(Romans 8:28)**. Our faith in Christ enables us to see beyond our present circumstances and hold on to the eternal perspective.

Moreover, as we persevere through trials, we can grow in our faith and character. **James 1:3–4** tells us that testing our faith produces perseverance and when it has finished its work, it makes us mature and complete, lacking nothing. Through trials, our faith is refined, our trust in God deepens, and our resilience is strengthened.

Finally, as believers, we find hope and encouragement in our ultimate victory in Christ. Jesus overcame the world and conquered sin and death through His death and resurrection. We are assured of His triumph, and we can rest in the knowledge that one day, all suffering and trials will cease, and we will be with Him for eternity.

So as a believer, I acknowledge that persevering through trials is a challenge, but I also embrace it as an opportunity for growth, faith, and a deeper relationship with God. I will press on with His strength and guidance, knowing that He is faithful to see me through every trial and that my hope ultimately rests in Him.

Overcoming Obstacles and Setbacks

As Christians, we believe that our journey in faith is not exempt from obstacles and setbacks. The calling of our faith often invites challenges and trials into our lives. However, through the grace of God and the power of Christ, we can find strength and perseverance to overcome these hurdles.

When faced with obstacles after answering the call of faith, it is important to remember that God is with us every step of the way. We can pray to Him, seeking His guidance and wisdom to navigate difficult times. The Bible reminds us in **Isaiah 41:10**, **"So do not fear, for I am with you; do not be dismayed, for I am your God. I will strengthen you and help you; I will uphold you with my righteous right hand." (NIV)**

In these moments, we must also remember the example set by Jesus Christ. He faced numerous obstacles and setbacks during His earthly ministry, yet He remained steadfast in His faith and fulfilled His purpose. We can draw inspiration from His perseverance and rely on His teachings to guide us through our challenges.

Moreover, the Christian community plays a vital role in supporting and encouraging one another. We are called to bear one another's burdens and offer a helping hand to those in need. Through fellowship, prayer, and sharing our faith journeys, we can find strength and encouragement to overcome obstacles together.

Cultivating an unwavering trust in God's plan for our lives is also essential. **Proverbs 3:5–6** reminds us, **"Trust in the Lord with all your heart and lean not on your understanding; in all your ways submit to him, and he will make your paths straight." (NIV)** Even when we face setbacks or encounter unexpected roadblocks, we can trust that God is working all things together for our good **(Romans 8:28)**.

Finally, maintaining a spirit of gratitude and praise can help us overcome obstacles with a renewed perspective. By focusing on the blessings we have received and praising God for His faithfulness, we can shift our attention away from the setbacks and instead fix our gaze upon the goodness of our Heavenly Father.

CHAPTER FIVE

Learning How to Activate "Now Faith" Through Our Challenges

Faith is an essential component of our Christian walk. It is the unwavering belief in the promises of God and the confident assurance of things hoped for, even when circumstances seem discouraging or overwhelming. Through faith, we can experience the power and presence of God working in and through us.

However, activating our faith is not always easy, especially in adversity. It takes deliberate effort and a commitment to believe in God's goodness and sovereignty even when everything suggests otherwise. Our difficulties serve as a training ground for our faith, allowing us to grow and deepen in our connection with God.

Developing a Strong Prayer Life

Developing a strong prayer life as a Christian is essential to activating and growing in faith, especially during challenging times. Prayer is a wonderful instrument for communicating with God, seeking His guidance, finding consolation, and developing a stronger connection with Him.

Here are some key steps to help you strengthen your prayer life and activate your faith:

- Recognize the importance of prayer. Prayer is not merely a religious ritual, but a personal connection with God. Recognize that

God desires to have a relationship with you and that prayer is a means to foster that relationship.

- Set aside dedicated time. Establish a regular time and place for prayer. This helps create a consistent habit and demonstrates your commitment to seeking God. It could be in the morning, before bed, or any other time that works best for you. Find a quiet and uninterrupted space where you can focus on prayer.

- Study the Scriptures. The Bible is vital for understanding God's character, promises, and teachings. Spend time reading and studying the Word of God to gain insight into His will and to be able to pray according to His Word. Scripture will guide your prayers and align them with God's purposes.

- Pray with faith. Approach prayer with confidence and faith, believing that God hears and answers your prayers. Trust that He is attentive to your needs and that His timing is perfect. As Jesus said in **Mark 11:24, "Therefore I tell you, whatever you ask in prayer, believe that you have received it, and it will be yours." (NIV)**

- Be honest and transparent. Prayer is a safe space to pour your heart into God. Be open and honest about your joys, struggles, fears, and doubts. Share your desires, hopes, and dreams with Him. God already knows your innermost thoughts but expressing them in prayer helps build intimacy and trust in your relationship with Him.

- Practice different types of prayer. Explore different methods to keep your prayer life dynamic. Besides regular conversation with God, you can engage in intercessory prayer (praying for others), thanksgiving and praise, repentance, and listening to God's voice through contemplative prayer.

- Seek fellowship and accountability. Engage with other believers who can support and encourage you in prayer. Join a prayer group or partner with a prayer buddy to share requests, pray together, and hold each other accountable. Corporate prayer can be particularly powerful and uplifting.

- Be persistent and patient. Faith and prayer are not about instant gratification. Sometimes, God may answer your prayers immediately, but other times, He may have different plans or timelines. Be persistent in prayer, trusting that God is working behind the scenes and His ways are higher than ours **(Isaiah 55:8–9)**.

- Reflect and journal. Reflect on your prayers and record how God answers them. Journaling helps you remember God's faithfulness and provides a tangible reminder of His work. It also allows you to see patterns and growth in your prayer journey.

- Trust in God's sovereignty. Remember that God is in control, even amid challenges. Trust His wisdom and sovereignty, knowing that He works all things together for the good of those who love Him **(Romans 8:28)**.

By implementing these practices consistently, you can deepen your prayer life, activate your faith, and experience the transformative power of prayer in the face of challenges.

Cultivating a Personal Relationship with God

Cultivating a personal relationship with God is a deeply meaningful and transformative journey that can help you activate and strengthen your faith, especially during challenging times. Here are some steps you can take to deepen your relationship with God and cultivate a vibrant faith:

- Seek God through prayer. A prayer is a powerful communication tool. Set aside dedicated time each day to pray and talk to God. Pour out your heart, express your joys, concerns, and challenges, and seek His guidance and wisdom. Through prayer,

you can develop a deeper connection with God and experience
His presence.

- Study and meditate on Scripture. The Bible is a precious source
of spiritual nourishment. Take time to study and meditate on its
teachings. Read passages that resonate with your current challenges and reflect on how they apply to your life. Allow God's
Word to speak to your heart and guide your thoughts, decisions,
and actions.

- Attend worship services and join a faith community. Regular
attendance at worship services and membership in a religious
based community can provide support, encouragement, and opportunity for growth. Engage in meaningful worship, listen to
inspiring sermons, and connect with fellow believers who can
share their experiences and insights. You can learn, grow, and
support one another on your spiritual journeys.

- Practice gratitude and praise. Cultivate gratitude by recognizing
and appreciating God's blessings. Daily, thank Him for His provision, guidance, and faithfulness. Expressing gratitude opens
your heart to God's presence and reinforces your trust. Praising
God through worship, song, and thanksgiving also helps foster a
deeper connection with Him.

- Trust and surrender to God's plan. In times of challenges, it can
be difficult to understand God's purposes and timing. However, trusting and surrendering to His plan can strengthen your
faith. Remember that God works for your ultimate good, even
when the path is difficult. Trust His wisdom and guidance, surrender your worries and fears to Him, and allow Him to lead you
through the challenges.

- Seek spiritual guidance and mentors. Consider seeking guidance
from spiritual leaders, mentors, or trusted individuals who can

offer insights and support as you navigate your faith journey. They can provide guidance, offer different perspectives, and help you deepen your understanding of God's Word.

- Practice patience and perseverance. Developing a personal relationship with God is a lifelong journey that requires patience and perseverance. Understand that faith grows gradually, and there will be ups and downs. Trust in God's timing and remain committed to cultivating your relationship with Him, even when faced with challenges.

CHAPTER SIX

Learning to Apply "Now Faith" as a Christian

As a Christian, living out your faith is not just about belief in Jesus Christ, but also about applying that faith in your everyday life. It's about taking your beliefs and putting them into action, allowing your faith to shape your thoughts, decisions, and actions. This process of applying your faith is often referred to as "living by faith" or "walking in faith."

Applying your faith is a continuous journey of growth and learning. It involves aligning your life with the teachings and principles found in the Bible, seeking a deeper relationship with God, and allowing the Holy Spirit to guide and transform you. It's important to note that applying your faith is not about earning your salvation or trying to be perfect but responding to God's grace and love by living in obedience to His Word.

Living a Life of Obedience to God's Commands

As Christians, we are called to be obedient to God's commandments. But how do we obey God's commandments through faith? In the following paragraphs, we will explore each of these topics in detail, providing practical guidance on how to obey God's commandments so that we can live in complete obedience and honor to God, our Creator.

Understanding God's commandments is the first and most crucial step toward obedience. As Christians, we must read, study, and meditate on God's Word to understand his commandments. **2 Timothy 3:16** declares that **"All scripture is given by inspiration of God, and is**

profitable for doctrine, for reproof, for correction, for instruction in righteousness." (KJV)

We can understand God's commandments by studying the Bible thoroughly. Reading the Bible regularly and applying its teachings to our daily lives is important. By doing so, we can understand and apply God's commandments to our lives.

Have Faith and Trust in God

Faith and obedience go hand in hand. We cannot effectively obey God's commandments without faith. The Bible says in **Hebrews 11:6, "But without faith it is impossible to please him: for he that cometh to God must believe that he is, And that he is a rewarder of them that diligently seek him." (KJV)**

We must have faith and trust in the Word of God, knowing that everything He commands is for our good. When we have faith and trust in God, we can obey His commands, knowing He has our best interests at heart.

Trusting God's Promises in All Areas of Life

The Bible constantly gives us images to help us visualize the character of God. **Psalm 18:2** says, **"The Lord is my rock, and my fortress, and my deliverer; my God, my strength, in whom I will trust; my buckler, and the horn of my salvation, and my high tower." (KJV) 2 Samuel 22:32 says, "For who is God, save the Lord? and who is a rock, save our God?" (KJV)** I love how the Lord uses creation to speak to us about the invisible attributes of his nature. In our eyes, the rocks are immutable, firm, and stable. Generations of men come and go, but the rocks remain visually the same. So it is also with our God. **1 Kings 8:56** says, **"Blessed be the Lord, that hath given rest unto his people Israel, according to all that he promised: there hath not failed one word of**

all his good promise, which he promised by the hand of Moses his servant." (KJV) God's promises are sure. They are even more immovable than the strongest mountains. They are firmer than the very ground you walk on.

You can trust God and believe that he will keep his promises. In fact, experiencing his promises the way God intended for you requires trust. **Isaiah 26:3–4** says, **"Thou wilt keep him in perfect peace, whose mind is stayed on thee: because he trusteth in thee. Trust ye in the Lord for ever: for in the Lord JEHOVAH is everlasting strength…" (KJV)** Throughout the Bible, God leads his people to peace. He has promised peace to us as his children. But **Isaiah 26** tells us about an incredibly important concept. Those who will remain in **"perfect peace"** are those **"of firm character,"** whose mind is kept on God. And a mind can only remain on God **"because [it] trusts."**

Experiencing the fullness of God's promises requires our unwavering trust. For example, **Philippians 4:19** says, **"But my God shall supply all your need according to his riches in glory by Christ Jesus." (KJV)** God promises to provide everything you need. His promise is sure. But experiencing the peace His promise of provision provides requires trusting His Word. He will provide for your needs regardless of your trust, but you will not be able to experience the peace God desires to give you if you are constantly worried about whether or not you will have everything you need. The commonly quoted promise from **Jeremiah 29:11** reads: **"For I know the thoughts that I think toward you, saith the Lord, thoughts of peace, and not of evil, to give you an expected end." (KJV)** God has an incredible plan for your life regardless of whether you trust His Word. But God's promise is meant to produce in you unshakable security. You are created to live your life trusting that God has a plan for you and will reveal it to you perfectly. Experiencing that security requires the act of trusting in God's character and His ability to guide you.

In what things do you need perfect peace today? In what areas do you need rest for your soul? Seek God's promises; remember that His promises are sure. He is your rock and your refuge. Put your trust in His promises as often as necessary until they produce peace.

Stepping Out in Faith and Taking Action

Stepping out in faith and taking action can be a powerful and transformative experience. It involves trusting your instincts, beliefs, and values and consciously deciding to pursue your goals or dreams. Here are a few key points to consider when stepping out in faith and taking action:

- Clarify your goals. Before taking action, you must clearly understand what you want to achieve. Take the time to reflect on your values, passions, and aspirations. Define your goals and create a roadmap for yourself.

- Overcome fear and doubt. Stepping out in faith often requires confronting fear and doubt. It's natural to feel uncertain or anxious when venturing into the unknown. Acknowledge your fears, but don't let them paralyze you. Cultivate self-belief, focus on your strengths, and remind yourself of past successes and resilience.

- Start small. Taking action doesn't always mean making grand gestures. Start with small steps toward your goal. Break down your larger goals into manageable tasks or milestones. Taking consistent action, no matter how small, builds momentum and confidence.

- Embrace failure as a learning opportunity. Understand that setbacks and failures are natural processes. Instead of viewing them as reasons to quit, see them as opportunities to learn, grow, and adjust your approach. Failure can provide valuable lessons and pave the way for future success.

- Seek support and guidance. Surround yourself with a supportive network of family, friends, mentors, or like-minded individuals who can provide encouragement, advice, and accountability. They can offer guidance, share their experiences, and provide valuable insights along your journey.

- Stay committed and persevere. Stepping out in faith requires persistence and determination. There may be obstacles, challenges, or moments of self-doubt along the way. Stay committed to your vision, remind yourself of your purpose, and persevere through difficulties. Consistency and resilience are key to achieving long-term success.

- Celebrate progress. As you take action and make progress, remember to celebrate your achievements, no matter how small. Recognize and appreciate the steps you've taken and the milestones you've reached. Celebrating your progress boosts motivation and reinforces your belief in your abilities.

Remember, stepping out in faith and taking action is a personal journey. Embrace the process, trust yourself, and believe in your ability to change your life positively.

CHAPTER SEVEN

Learning to Walk in "Now Faith" as a Leader

In today's rapidly changing world, leadership is necessary to navigate complex challenges and achieve success. However, more than conventional leadership practices may be required to drive innovation, inspire followers, and achieve extraordinary outcomes. As a result, there is a growing interest in exploring new perspectives of leadership that emphasize the importance of faith, particularly "Now Faith," as a transformative element in the leadership process.

1. Embrace uncertainty. As a leader, you will encounter situations where the outcome is uncertain. Instead of being paralyzed by fear or doubt, embrace the unknown and view it as an opportunity for growth and learning. Trust that you have the necessary skills and resources to adapt and find solutions.

2. Develop a clear vision. A leader with "Now Faith" has a clear vision of where they lead their team. Communicate this vision to your team members, inspiring them to align their efforts toward a common goal. A strong vision provides a sense of purpose and direction, fueling motivation and confidence.

3. Foster a positive mindset. Cultivate an optimistic mindset within yourself and your team. Encourage a can-do attitude, emphasizing the potential for success rather than dwelling on potential failures. Positivity creates an environment where everyone feels empowered and motivated to take action.

4. Take calculated risks. Faith requires a willingness to take calculated risks. Evaluate the benefits and consequences of different actions and make informed decisions. Be willing to stretch yourself and encourage your team members to do the same. Learn from your mistakes and turn them into chances for progress.

5. Lead by example. Demonstrate "Now Faith" by leading with integrity, authenticity, and transparency. Show your team that you trust and believe in their abilities, empowering them to take ownership and make decisions. Be open to feedback and actively seek input from your team members to foster a culture of collaboration and innovation.

Leading by Example and Inspiring Others

Leading by example and inspiring others through faith is a powerful way to impact individuals and communities positively. Living your faith openly and genuinely can serve as a source of inspiration and motivation for others to do the same. Here are a few key aspects to consider when seeking to lead by example and inspire others through faith:

1. Live your values. Ensure that your actions align with the principles and values of your faith. Act with integrity, compassion, kindness, and humility. By consistently demonstrating these qualities daily, you set an example that others can admire and emulate.

2. Be inclusive and accepting. Embrace diversity and demonstrate inclusivity in your interactions. Treat everyone with respect and love, regardless of background, beliefs, or circumstances. By fostering an environment of acceptance, you create space for others to feel valued and appreciated.

3. Share your journey. Be open and transparent about your faith journey. Share your experiences, struggles, and how your faith has positively impacted your life. When people see the transformative power of faith in their own life, they may find encouragement and inspiration for their spiritual growth.

4. Serve others selflessly. Actively engage in acts of service and seek opportunities to help those in need. By demonstrating a selfless attitude and a willingness to lend a hand, you can inspire others to do the same. Your actions can serve as a tangible expression of your faith and provide a practical example for others.

5. Cultivate meaningful relationships. Foster deep and meaningful connections with others. Listen attentively, offer support, and provide encouragement to those around you. Building strong relationships based on trust and love can create an environment where faith is shared and individuals can support and inspire one another.

6. Be a source of hope and encouragement. Demonstrate unwavering faith and hope in times of adversity. Maintaining a positive outlook and trusting in a higher power can inspire others to do the same. Your resilience and optimism can be a guiding light during challenging circumstances.

Remember that leading by example and inspiring others through faith is ongoing. It requires consistent effort, self-reflection, and a genuine desire to make a difference. By embodying your faith in your everyday life, you have the potential to positively impact those around you and create a ripple effect of inspiration and transformation.

Making Decisions Based on Faith, Not Fear

As a leader, walking in faith and making decisions based on trust and belief is essential rather than succumbing to fear and doubt. By following these biblical principles, you can cultivate a mindset of unwavering faith:

1. Deepen your spiritual foundation. Dedicate time to prayer, meditation, and studying the Word of God. Build a solid relationship with your Creator, aligning your decisions with His teachings and wisdom.

2. Seek divine wisdom. Approach decision-making with a humble heart, seeking guidance from God through prayer and counsel from wise mentors and spiritual advisors. Allow His wisdom to illuminate your path.

3. Identify fear-based thinking. Be alert to negative thoughts rooted in fear and doubt. Replace them with affirmations of faith and trust in God's promises. Declare His truth over your life and decisions.

4. Embrace your purpose. Clarify your vision as a leader and understand how it aligns with God's purpose for your life. Let your decisions be driven by a desire to fulfill His plan, trusting that He will equip you for the journey.

5. Embrace uncertainty. Recognize that uncertainty is an opportunity for growth and reliance on God. Step out in faith, knowing that He is with you every step of the way. Trust His sovereignty, even when the path seems unclear.

6. Cultivate gratitude and mindfulness. Develop a heart of gratitude, acknowledging God's goodness and faithfulness. Stay mindful of the present moment, attuned to His guidance and the needs of those you lead.

7. Reflect on God's faithfulness. Recall past instances where God has shown His faithfulness in your life. Remember His provisions, guidance, and miracles.

Equipping and Empowering Others to Walk in Faith

According to the Word of God, equipping and empowering others to walk in faith is an important aspect of Christian discipleship. The Bible provides guidance and principles that can help us understand this concept and put it into practice. Let's explore key passages highlighting the significance of equipping and empowering others in their faith journey.

Ephesians 4:11–12

So Christ himself gave the apostles, the prophets, the evangelists, the pastors and teachers, to equip his people for works of service, so that the body of Christ may be built up. (NIV)

This verse emphasizes that Christ has given leaders and teachers within the Church to equip believers for service. The purpose of this equipping is to build up the body of Christ. As followers of Jesus, we are responsible for equipping and empowering one another to walk in faith, using our gifts and abilities to serve and strengthen the Church.

2 Timothy 2:2

And the things you have heard me say in the presence of many witnesses entrust to reliable people who will also be qualified to teach others. (NIV)

Here, the apostle Paul instructs Timothy to pass on the teachings and truths of the faith to reliable individuals who can, in turn, teach others. This verse emphasizes the importance of a generational transfer of faith and knowledge. We are called to invest in others, sharing what we have learned and empowering them to do the same with future generations.

Matthew 28:19-20

Therefore go and make disciples of all nations, baptizing them in the name of the Father and of the Son and of the Holy Spirit, and teaching them to obey everything I have commanded you. (NIV)

Known as the Great Commission, this passage highlights Jesus's mission to His disciples. Making disciples involves sharing the Gospel and teaching and guiding them in their journey of faith. By equipping others to obey God's commandments and teaching them to walk in faith, we fulfill this commission and contribute to the growth of God's kingdom.

Hebrews 10:24-25

And let us consider how we may spur one another on toward love and good deeds, not giving up meeting together, as some are in the habit of doing, but encouraging one another—and all the more as you see the Day approaching. (NIV)

This verse encourages believers to actively engage in uplifting one another. We are called to encourage and spur each other toward love and good deeds. By meeting together, supporting one another, and providing encouragement, we can empower others to walk in faith, especially when faith may be tested.

God instructs us to equip and empower others to walk in faith. We are called to teach, mentor, encourage, and support fellow believers, enabling them to grow in their relationship with God, serve the Church, and impact the world around them. By following these principles, we fulfill the Great Commission and build up the body of Christ.

CHAPTER EIGHT

Having "Now Faith" Doesn't Always Change Your Direction

Faith or belief in something does not guarantee a change in direction or outcome. Faith is often associated with trust and confidence in a belief or system. While it can provide motivation and hope, it does not necessarily alter the external circumstances or events in one's life.

Faith can significantly shape one's perspective and mindset, influencing decision-making and actions. It can provide emotional strength, resilience, and a sense of purpose during challenging times. However, it is important to acknowledge that external factors, such as opportunities, resources, and the choices of others, can still impact the direction of one's life, regardless of the strength of their faith.

Understanding God's Sovereignty During Challenges

Believers often face an array of challenges in their lives, prompting them to seek solace and guidance from their faith. One concept that holds significant importance in such circumstances is understanding God's sovereignty. Here are a few key points to consider:

1. God's sovereignty. God's sovereignty refers to His supreme power and authority over all things. It means that God controls everything that happens in the world, including our challenges. Recognizing God's sovereignty involves understanding that He

has a plan and purpose for everything, even if we can't always comprehend it.

2. Trusting in God's wisdom. Challenges can be perplexing, and it's natural to question why certain things happen. However, acknowledging God's sovereignty means trusting His wisdom and understanding that His ways are higher than ours. This trust can help us find peace and hope amid difficult circumstances, knowing God is working out His purposes.

3. The presence of free will. While God is sovereign, He has also granted humans free will. Our choices and actions can have consequences that impact our lives and the lives of others. Sometimes the challenges we face result from our own decisions or the actions of others. God's sovereignty doesn't negate our responsibility or the effects of free will.

4. God's promise of comfort and guidance. Amid challenges, God promises to be with us. He offers comfort, strength, and guidance through His presence and Word. Turning to prayer, seeking solace in Scriptures, and connecting with a supportive spiritual community can provide the reassurance needed to navigate difficult times.

5. Finding purpose in challenges. God can work through challenges to refine our character, strengthen our faith, and bring about growth and transformation. While seeing the purpose in adversity may be challenging, trusting in God's sovereignty gives us hope that He can bring something good out of difficult situations.

Remember that grappling with the concept of God's sovereignty in the face of challenges is a deeply personal process. Seeking direction from recognized spiritual leaders or mentors who can provide knowledge and support during this journey can be beneficial.

Finding Peace and Contentment in God's Plan

As mentioned, faith means "finding peace and contentment in God's plan." It is a concept rooted in religious beliefs, particularly within Christianity. The Bible teaches that faith is essential to a believer's relationship with God.

In the Bible, the Book of Hebrews defines faith as **"the assurance of things hoped for, the conviction of things not seen." (Hebrews 11:1, ESV)** It emphasizes that faith involves trusting in God and His promises, even when circumstances may seem uncertain or challenging.

There are several examples of people who displayed confidence in God throughout the Bible. For instance, Abraham believed God's promise that he would become the Father of many nations, despite being old and childless at the time. Noah faithfully obeyed God's command to build an ark, even though there had been no rain. These stories highlight the importance of trusting in God's plan and having faith in His guidance.

Faith also involves finding peace and contentment in God's plan, even when it doesn't align with our desires or understanding. It means surrendering our will and acknowledging that God's ways are higher than ours **(Isaiah 55:9)**. It requires believing that God is in control and that His plan is ultimately for our good, even if we cannot fully comprehend it.

By cultivating faith, believers seek to deepen their relationship with God, finding solace, peace, and contentment in His presence. Faith helps individuals navigate life's challenges, lean on God's strength, and trust that He will work all things together for their benefit **(Romans 8:28)**.

It's important to note that faith is a personal journey, and individuals may have different interpretations and expressions of their faith. The Bible guides understanding and nurturing faith, providing principles and teachings to support believers in their quest for peace and contentment in God's plan.

Trusting God's Wisdom and Guidance, Even When It Doesn't Align with Our Expectations

Trusting God's wisdom and guidance, even when it doesn't align with our expectations, can be a challenging but rewarding aspect of faith. It requires a deep belief that God's plans are ultimately for our good, even if they differ from what we desire or anticipate. Here are a few key points to consider when facing such situations:

1. Understanding God's Sovereignty

Recognize that God is all-knowing and all-powerful. His understanding surpasses our limited human comprehension, and His plans are often beyond our understanding. Trusting in His wisdom means acknowledging He sees the bigger picture and has a perfect plan for our lives, even if it doesn't match our expectations.

2. Developing Patience and Surrender

Trusting God's guidance involves surrendering our desires and plans to Him. It means embracing the possibility that His timing and methods might be different from what we envision. This requires humility and a willingness to let go of control, acknowledging that God's ways are higher than our ways.

3. Seeking God's Perspective

Spend time in prayer and reflection, seeking God's perspective on the situation. Communicate honestly with Him, sharing your hopes, fears, and doubts. Ask for guidance and wisdom, and be open to receiving His answers, even if they differ from what you anticipated. God often speaks to us through Scripture, so reading and meditating on His Word can provide clarity and direction.

4. Trusting God's Faithfulness

Reflect on your past experiences of God's faithfulness and provision. Remember how He has guided you through difficult times and how His plans, though initially challenging, ultimately brought about blessings and growth. Remind yourself of His promises and trust that He will remain faithful in the present and future.

5. Embracing Faith and Growth

Trusting God's wisdom and guidance, even when it contradicts our expectations, requires faith and a willingness to grow spiritually. It may entail pushing ourselves out of our comfort zones, taking risks, and embracing uncertainty. Remember that God frequently uses unexpected events to develop us and pull us closer to Him. Embracing these growth opportunities can lead to deeper faith and a stronger relationship with God.

Ultimately, trusting God's wisdom and guidance means surrendering our expectations, embracing His plans, and aligning our will with His. It requires faith, patience, and an unwavering belief that God's ways are perfect, even when they don't align with our own. Through this trust, we can experience His peace and find joy in the journey, knowing He is always with us.

CHAPTER NINE

Understanding Why God Chose You for the Storm

When you go through a storm, God is not distant or indifferent. He is the "I Am" and works in your life for your benefit. If you feel like you're going under a storm. Have courage because Jesus is with you. Don't even consider fear. When fear wants to come, tell it where to go. Let it argue with Jesus!

Take a leap of faith. Don't ask God to bless your efforts. Do what God has blessed you to do. Ask him what he wants you to do and prepare to get off the boat.

Maintain Your Focus on Jesus

The moment you take your eyes off the Lord, you will sink. **Matthew 14:30** says, **"But when he saw the wind boisterous, he was afraid; and beginning to sink, he cried, saying, Lord, save me." (KJV)** When you concentrate on the wind and waves—your circumstances—you will sink, just like Peter. When you look at the world, you will be distressed. When you look within yourself, you will be dejected. But when you look to Christ, you will be at peace.

You don't need great faith to weather the storms in your life. You need to have faith in the right person. Even in the storm, even when you feel like you're sinking, even when you're scared to death, worship God all the time. Thank Him in the middle of the storm.

He is allowing you to go through this storm for the same reason He sent the disciples into the storm to say, "I am all you need. I can handle anything. And I will come walking on what you fear the most. I'm not asking you to come to me. I will go to you."

Recognizing God's Purpose in Difficult Seasons

They are almost always linked to our relationships, economic situation, family, health, or professional career. Sometimes it is difficult for us to understand why these tests have occurred. At such times, we may feel overwhelmed, confused, and alone.

While we are in the midst of trials, we cannot understand what God wants to achieve through these difficulties. The Bible assures us that the Lord wants the best for our lives and will work even in the most difficult times for our good.

Understanding the difference between walking in the dark and facing dark times is vital. As believers in Christ, we do not live in the darkness of sin **(Colossians 1:13)**. However, in order for us to be molded, the Lord allows us to face trials and tribulations. In the story of Joseph in **Genesis 37–39,** we find six principles that we can remember in times of trouble:

1. God is with Us in Difficult Times

This is the foundation to be able to face the tests. Guided by his jealousy, Joseph's brothers plotted to assassinate him, but the Lord touched the hearts of Ruben and Judah **(Genesis 37:21, 26)**. The Bible affirms that God was with Joseph at all times, from when he was sold as an enslaved person until his imprisonment. The Lord prospered him and gave him favor before Pharaoh **(Genesis 39:2–6, 21–23)**. In **Hebrews 13:5,** God declares, **"I will never leave thee, nor forsake thee." (KJV)** There is no place so far away, no difficulty too great for us to be out of the reach of our Heavenly Father **(Psalm 139:7–12)**.

2. God Allows Hard Times for a Reason

No matter how difficult the test seems, if you follow Jesus Christ, God has a good reason for allowing that difficulty in your life. Joseph was seventeen years old when he was sold into slavery, and it was not until he was thirty that he became governor of Egypt. So for thirteen years, he had to face adversity.

Sometimes when we suffer grievances, we divert our attention from God to focus on the situation we are facing or on the people who have mistreated us. The Lord had a purpose with every step Joseph took on his rocky path. In God's plans, Joseph would save not only his family, but all of Egypt during the seven years of famine. That is why Joseph tells his brothers: **"But as for you, ye thought evil against me; but God meant it unto good, to bring to pass, as it is this day, to save much people alive." (Genesis 50:20, KJV)** God's sovereign direction in the life of Joseph illustrates the truth that **Romans 8:28** teaches us: **"And we know that all things work together for good to those who love God, to those who are the called according to his purpose." (NKJV)**

3. The Darkness Will Last as Long as It Takes for God to Fulfill His Purpose

We all get impatient in moments of pain. But if we could see the future during darkness, we would thank the Lord, for we would understand the purpose of his trials. In the midst of what Joseph suffered at Potiphar's house and in prison, he learned the Egyptian language and its customs. And in addition, he acquired administrative skills, learned to live under authority, and knew how to supervise others. God prepared him so he would have a wonderful place of service as second in command after Pharaoh.

The Lord never showed him His plan and the time it would happen. So even if we would like to shorten the tests, we have to recognize that the difficulties shape us. Let's not battle against God. Rather, let us surrender our will by saying, "Lord, I do not understand this, nor is it to my liking, but I surrender to your purpose, whatever it may be. Keep me in this place until you make it."

4.   Often, We Learn More in the Dark Than in the Light

No matter where Joseph was, whether at the bottom of the cistern, in Potiphar's house, or in jail, he kept moving toward the light. All that time, God continued to direct him toward his divine purpose: Joseph would become governor of Egypt. His plan would save not only Joseph's family, but the entire population of Egypt. His story would be written in the Bible for teaching and blessing.

We all want to avoid learning through difficulties, but the lessons are only acquired once we go through the trials. Experiencing our complete dependence on God amid tribulations is far more effective than just hearing about His faithfulness.

5.   Even in Dark Moments, We Walk Toward the Light
Be not wise in thine own eyes: fear the Lord, and depart from evil. (Proverb 3:7, KJV)

God has a perfect plan for our lives. We can fulfill His plan by trusting Him and following Him in obedience. We must obey Him even when making the right decision is difficult or involves a sacrifice. Why? Because this is how our Heavenly Father molds our character. Only faithful obedience allows us to grow in wisdom and maturity to serve Him. If you can't see the light at the end of the tunnel, you may be looking in the wrong direction. Do not focus on the darkness; fix your eyes on the Lord. He will not illuminate the entire path at the same time but will illuminate enough for us to take one step at a time **(Psalm 119:105***)*.

6. What We Learn in the Dark, We Must Share in the Light

Joseph had grown up in a family that believed in Jehovah, but suddenly found himself in an idolatrous society. When interpreting Pharaoh's dream, he never tried to hide his faith in the one true God (**Genesis 41:1, 25, 28, 32**).

The Lord has been building his principles in your life and wants you to share these truths with others. Many of those who walk around us live in darkness, vanity, anxiety, and frustration. But you must make His life available to your neighbor and the lessons you have learned in the darkest moments.

Growing Spiritually Through Trials

According to the Bible, trials and hardships can serve as spiritual growth and development opportunities. The Scriptures are a guide for navigating through difficult times, finding strength, and growing closer to God.

Recognize that God is in control of all things, even your trials. Trust that He has a purpose and a plan for your life, even amid difficult circumstances. **Proverbs 3:5–6** says, **"Trust in the Lord with all your heart and do not lean on your understanding. In all your ways, acknowledge him, and he will make straight your paths." (ESV)**

- Persevere with endurance. Endurance is developed through perseverance in trials. **James 1:2–4** encourages believers to consider it joy when they face trials because they produce endurance, which leads to maturity and completeness. Keep pressing, knowing God can use your trials to build character and develop faith.
- Seek God's wisdom. When going through trials, seek wisdom from God. **James 1:5** says, **"If any of you lacks wisdom, let him ask God, who gives generously to all without reproach,**

and it will be given him." (ESV) Ask God for guidance, clarity, and understanding amid your difficulties.

- Find comfort in God's presence. Turn to God for comfort and solace during challenging times. **Psalm 34:18** assures us that the Lord is near to the brokenhearted and saves the crushed in spirit. Spend time in prayer, read His Word, and lean on His promises. Seek solace in His presence and let Him bring you peace.

- Allow trials to refine your character. Trials can refine and purify your character, producing spiritual growth. **Romans 5:3–4** says, **"Not only that, but we rejoice in our sufferings, knowing that suffering produces endurance, and endurance produces character, and character produces hope." (ESV)** Embrace the opportunity to grow in patience, perseverance, and faithfulness.

- Find strength in the community. Surround yourself with fellow believers who can offer support, encouragement, and prayer during difficult times. **Galatians 6:2** urges us to bear one another's burdens, and **Hebrews 10:24–25** encourages us to meet together, encourage one another, and spur each other on to love and do good deeds.

- Cultivate an attitude of gratitude. Despite the trials, maintain an attitude of gratitude, focusing on the blessings and goodness of God. **1 Thessalonians 5:18** instructs us to give thanks in all circumstances. Gratitude helps shift our perspective and opens our hearts to God's faithfulness, even amid trials.

Remember that everyone's journey is unique, and God works differently in each person's life. Embrace the challenges as opportunities for growth and trust in God's faithfulness through it all.

Encouraging Others Through Your Own Experiences

Sharing your experiences with others can be an effective method to motivate and inspire them. Here are some ideas to get you started:

1. Be authentic. Share your experiences honestly and openly. People appreciate authenticity and can connect more deeply when they sense you're genuine.

2. Overcome challenges. Talk about your obstacles and how you overcame them. Sharing the difficulties you encountered and the strategies you used to overcome them can inspire others to persist in their challenges.

3. Highlight personal growth. Discuss how certain experiences or setbacks helped you grow as a person. Emphasize the positive lessons you learned from difficult situations and how they shaped you into a stronger individual.

4. Focus on resilience. Share stories about how you bounced back from failures or setbacks. Highlight the importance of resilience and how it helped you navigate tough times. Encourage others to cultivate resilience in their own lives.

5. Celebrate small victories. Share your accomplishments, no matter how small they may seem. By celebrating your victories, you can inspire others to appreciate their progress and achievements, no matter how insignificant they might initially appear.

6. Provide practical advice. Offer practical tips and strategies based on your experiences. Share the specific actions or mindset shifts that helped you overcome challenges or achieve success. Practical advice can be empowering and actionable for others.

7. Show empathy and support. Remember to empathize with others and offer support. Encouragement is not just about sharing your own experiences; it's also about being there for others, listening to their struggles, and offering comfort and guidance.

Everyone's journey is unique, and what worked for you may only work for some. However, by sharing your experiences and offering encouragement, you can provide valuable insights, inspiration, and motivation to those facing similar challenges.

CHAPTER TEN

Learn to Always Trust God, Not Your Faith

Trusting God and having faith are often intertwined, as they both involve a belief in a higher power and the willingness to rely on that power for guidance and support. However, it's important to understand that trusting God and trusting your faith are not mutually exclusive. They can profoundly complement each other.

Faith can be seen as the foundation of your relationship with God. It is the belief in things not seen and the assurance of things hoped for. It is a personal, inner conviction that allows you to surrender control and place your trust in God's wisdom, love, and provision. Faith helps you navigate difficult times, strengthens you, and deepens your connection with the divine. Trusting God means recognizing His sovereignty, goodness, and plans for your life. It involves surrendering your desires and understanding that God's ways may not always align with yours.

Trusting God requires humility, patience, and a willingness to let go of your limited perspective to embrace His greater wisdom. However, it's important to remember that faith is not a magical formula and does not guarantee specific outcomes. Sometimes, our faith may be tested, and we may not fully understand why certain things happen. It is during these moments that trusting God becomes crucial.

Differentiation Between Faith and Faithfulness

According to the Bible, faith and faithfulness are related concepts but have distinct meanings. Let's explore their definitions and differences based on biblical teachings.

Faith

In the Bible, faith is often described as trust, confidence, or belief in God and His promises. **Hebrews 11:1** provides a well-known definition: **"Now faith is the assurance of things hoped for, the conviction of things not seen." (ESV)** Faith involves believing in God's existence, character, Word, and ability to fulfill His promises. Through faith, people are justified before God and receive salvation **(Ephesians 2:8–9)**.

Faithfulness

Faithfulness, on the other hand, refers to the quality of being reliable, trustworthy, and steadfast. It is closely associated with loyalty and commitment. Faithfulness is often used in the Bible to describe God's character and actions. For example, **Deuteronomy 7:9** states, **"Know therefore that the Lord your God is God, the faithful God who keeps covenant and steadfast love with those who love him and keep his commandments." (ESV)**

Faithfulness is also expected from believers as a response to God's faithfulness. It involves remaining committed to God, obeying His commandments, and fulfilling one's responsibilities. In the New Testament, faithfulness is listed as a fruit of the Spirit **(Galatians 5:22)** and is praised as a virtue in various passages **(Matthew 25:21, 1 Corinthians 4:2)**.

While faith primarily focuses on trust and belief, faithfulness is about being steadfast and dependable in one's relationship with God and others. Faithfulness is a fruit of genuine faith and is demonstrated through obedience, loyalty, and consistent devotion.

Faith is the belief and trust in God, while faithfulness is the quality of being reliable and loyal in one's relationship with God and others. Faith leads to salvation, and faithfulness is the response and fruit of genuine faith. Both are important aspects of a believer's walk with God, highlighting the trust in His promises and the commitment to live according to His will.

Relying on God's Character and Faithfulness

As the Bible describes, relying on God's character and faithfulness is a central theme in the Christian faith. The Bible portrays God as loving, merciful, just, and trustworthy. Believers find comfort and strength in knowing God's character remains consistent and reliable throughout all circumstances.

God's character and faithfulness according to the Bible:

1. God's love and mercy. The Bible teaches that God is love (**1 John 4:8**) and that His mercy endures forever (**Psalm 136:1**). God's love is unconditional, and His mercy is extended to all who seek Him. Believers rely on God's love and mercy to find forgiveness, grace, and compassion in times of need.

2. God's faithfulness. The Bible emphasizes God's faithfulness in keeping His promises. Scripture affirms that God is faithful and trustworthy (**1 Corinthians 10:13, 2 Thessalonians 3:3**). This faithfulness extends to His covenant with His people, ensuring He will never abandon or forsake them (**Deuteronomy 31:6, Hebrews 13:5**).

3. God's provision and care. The Bible teaches that God provides for His creation and cares for His people. Jesus taught His followers not to worry about their basic needs, but to trust God's provision (**Matthew 6:25–34**). Believers rely on God's faithfulness to provide for their physical, emotional, and spiritual needs.

4. God's sovereignty and wisdom. The Bible affirms that God is sovereign and has ultimate control over all things **(Psalm 103:19)**. His wisdom is unfathomable, and His plans are perfect **(Romans 11:33–36)**. Relying on God's character means trusting His sovereign guidance and understanding that His ways are higher than ours **(Isaiah 55:8–9)**.

5. God's unchanging nature. The Bible teaches that God is immutable, meaning He does not change **(Malachi 3:6, James 1:17)**. His character remains consistent throughout time, providing a solid foundation for believers to rely on. In a constantly changing world, God's faithfulness and unchanging nature bring comfort and stability.

Relying on God's character and faithfulness involves developing a personal relationship through prayer, studying the Bible, and seeking His guidance. It means trusting that He is good, just, and true, even in the face of challenges or uncertainties. Believers find strength and hope in the assurance that God's character and faithfulness never waver, providing a firm foundation for their lives.

Letting Go of Self-Reliance and Surrendering to God's Will

Letting go of self-reliance and surrendering to God's will is a profound and personal journey that involves cultivating trust, faith, and humility. It is a process of acknowledging that there are limits to our control and understanding and recognizing that God can guide and support us.

Here are a few steps you can consider taking on this path:

1. Reflect on your beliefs. Contemplate your understanding of God and your relationship with Him. Explore your beliefs, values,

and spiritual traditions to clarify your connection to something beyond yourself.

2. Cultivate trust and surrender. Practice trusting in God and surrendering your desires, plans, and outcomes. This doesn't mean giving up responsibility or becoming passive; rather, it involves acknowledging that there is wisdom in surrendering to God and being open to His guidance.

3. Prayer and meditation. Engage in prayer or meditation practices that allow you to connect with God and seek His guidance. These practices can help calm the mind, open the heart, and create space for listening to the voice of God, which is the Holy Spirit within.

4. Letting go of ego. Self-reliance often stems from the ego's need to control and feel important. Letting go of self-reliance involves recognizing and releasing the ego's grip, embracing humility, and acknowledging that a pearl of greater wisdom is at play.

5. Seek spiritual guidance. If you feel drawn to it, seek guidance from spiritual mentors, teachers, or communities that align with your beliefs. They can offer support, share their experiences, and provide insights on surrendering to God's will.

6. Practice surrender in daily life. Embrace opportunities in your everyday life to practice surrendering to God's will. This can include accepting situations beyond your control, surrendering attachments, and trusting that everything is unfolding as it should, even if it doesn't align with your desires.

Remember, surrendering to God's will is a deeply personal journey that may look different for each individual. Allow yourself the time and space to explore and nurture your relationship with Him, and trust that the path will unfold in its own time.

CHAPTER ELEVEN

Understanding Your New Tool for the Journey

Faith plays a significant role in navigating life's challenges, providing strength and hope, and helping individuals overcome obstacles and grow spiritually. Let's explore these aspects in more detail. Faith, in Christianity, is a steadfast anchor during life's trials and tribulations. It offers believers a sense of purpose, meaning, and direction, guiding them through challenges with unwavering trust in God's plan. Christian faith centers around a personal relationship with Jesus Christ, seen as the ultimate source of strength, comfort, and guidance.

In Christianity, faith assures believers of God's presence and love, even amid adversity. It instills hope and optimism, allowing Christians to persevere through difficulties with confidence in God's faithfulness. Trusting in God's promises and His sovereignty brings inner peace and serenity, enabling Christians to face life's challenges with unwavering resolve.

Christian faith is deeply rooted in community and fellowship. Believers are encouraged to come together as the body of Christ, supporting and uplifting one another. The church serves as a source of spiritual guidance, offering encouragement, prayer, and practical assistance. The fellowship of believers provides a sense of belonging, reminding Christians that they are not alone in their struggles and can lean on one another for support.

Moreover, faith in Christ provides a moral compass for navigating ethical dilemmas. Christian beliefs are grounded in the teachings of Jesus, which emphasize love, compassion, forgiveness, and righteousness. These principles guide Christians in making choices that align with God's will and reflect their commitment to live a life of integrity and obedience to Him.

Christian faith also offers a profound sense of meaning and purpose. Believers understand that they are part of God's divine plan and that their lives have significance in His eyes. They find meaning in worshiping God, serving others, and spreading the gospel of Jesus Christ. This perspective gives Christians hope and motivation to persevere through challenges, knowing their lives have eternal significance.

The Christian faith brings solace and comfort in times of grief and loss. Believers find assurance in the hope of eternal life and the promise of reunion with loved ones in heaven. Christian rituals, such as prayer, reading Scripture, and participating in worship, provide a framework for processing grief and finding emotional healing in the presence of God.

Furthermore, faith in Christ encourages Christians to cultivate virtues and character traits that align with Christ's teachings. This includes demonstrating patience, compassion, forgiveness, and gratitude. These virtues enable believers to respond to challenges with Christlike grace, resilience, and empathy, reflecting the love of God in their actions and attitudes.

Embracing Faith as a Source of Strength and Hope

Faith provides strength and hope by instilling confidence, resilience, and optimism. Believing in something greater than oneself can empower individuals to face adversity with courage and determination. Faith can foster a deep inner conviction that there is a purpose and reason to persevere even amid hardship. It can offer solace, encouragement, and a sense of belonging to a community of like-minded individuals with similar beliefs and values.

Embracing Faith as a Source of Strength and Hope: A Biblical Perspective

In line with the teachings of the Bible, embracing faith becomes a deep wellspring of strength and unwavering hope for believers. The Scriptures guide cultivating faith and emphasize its transformative power in navigating life's challenges. Let us delve into this biblical perspective:

1. The Strength of Faith

Faith, according to the Bible, surpasses mere belief. It involves placing deep trust in God and His promises. **Hebrews 11:1** describes faith as **"the assurance of things hoped for, the conviction of things not seen." (ESV)** It entails unwavering reliance on God's character, Word, and faithfulness. Through this trust, believers can face trials with unwavering resolve.

2. Hope in God's Promises

Biblical faith enables individuals to find hope in the promises of God. **Romans 15:13** reminds us that God is the ultimate source of hope, filling believers with joy and peace as they trust Him. Faith allows Christians to find solace in God's love, mercy, and guidance, even during life's most challenging circumstances.

3. Overcoming Obstacles

The Bible emphasizes the power of faith to overcome obstacles. Jesus reassures His disciples in **John 16:33** saying, **"In this world you will have trouble. But take heart! I have overcome the world." (NIV)** Faith empowers believers to rely on God's strength and victory, knowing they can conquer adversity through Him.

4. Spiritual Growth

Faith plays a pivotal role in the spiritual growth of believers. It encourages individuals to deepen their relationship with God, seeking His wisdom, guidance, and understanding. **James 1:2–4** urges believers to view trials as opportunities for growth as they cultivate perseverance and maturity in their faith.

5. Communal Support

The Bible underscores the significance of community in nurturing faith. **Hebrews 10:24–25** encourages believers to gather together, providing support, encouragement, and mutual accountability. Through fellowship with fellow believers, individuals find strength and inspiration as they journey together in faith. By embracing the teachings of the Bible and cultivating faith, individuals can experience the transformative power of God's presence in their lives. Faith becomes a wellspring of strength, grounding believers in God's promises and bestowing unwavering hope. Through faith, believers can overcome obstacles, experience spiritual growth, and find support within the community of fellow believers, while deepening their relationship with God.

Applying Faith to Overcome Obstacles and Grow Spiritually

Applying faith to overcome obstacles and grow spiritually is a powerful practice that individuals across various religious and spiritual traditions have embraced. Faith can provide the strength, hope, and resilience needed to navigate challenges and deepen one's spiritual journey. Here are some ways you can apply faith to overcome obstacles and foster spiritual growth:

1. Trust in God. Have faith in God. Trust that this higher power is guiding and supporting you through difficult times. Surrender your worries and anxieties to Him, knowing that He has a greater plan for you.

2. Prayer and meditation. Engage in regular prayer or meditation practices to connect with your faith. These practices can help you find inner peace, clarity, and strength. Pray for guidance, strength, and the ability to overcome obstacles. Meditate to quiet your mind, deepen your spiritual awareness, and receive insights and inspiration.

3. Seek wisdom from Scriptures. Explore the teachings and wisdom of the Bible. It contains guidance, stories, and parables that can inspire and give insights into overcoming challenges. Reflect on the lessons and apply them to your life circumstances.

4. Surround yourself with a supportive community. Engage with like-minded individuals who share your faith or spiritual beliefs. Participate in religious services, spiritual gatherings, or support groups. Sharing your struggles and triumphs with others who understand and support your spiritual journey can provide encouragement and strength.

5. Practice gratitude. Cultivate a mindset of gratitude, even in the face of adversity. Recognize and appreciate the blessings in your life, no matter how small. Gratitude can shift your perspective, increase positivity, and deepen your connection to your faith.

6. Embrace challenges as opportunities for growth. View obstacles as personal and spiritual growth opportunities. Understand that challenges can be transformative experiences that strengthen your faith, resilience, and character. Have faith that you have the inner resources and support to overcome difficulties and emerge stronger on the other side.

7. Reflect and learn from past experiences. Reflect on obstacles you've overcome and how your faith played a role in those situations. Recognize the lessons you've learned and the growth you've experienced. Draw on these experiences as a reminder of your inner strength and ability to navigate future challenges with faith.

Remember, applying faith to overcome obstacles and grow spiritually is a personal journey, and everyone's path may be unique. Find what resonates with you and adapt these suggestions to align with your beliefs and practices. Ultimately, faith can be a source of strength, guidance, and transformation as you navigate life's challenges and deepen your spiritual connection.

Conclusion

In conclusion, understanding what faith is truly lays the foundation for a deeper relationship with God. It involves accepting and trusting in God's Word, which leads to a call for faith in our lives. However, challenges are inevitable after answering this call, and they serve as opportunities for growth and activating our faith. As Christians, it is crucial to apply "Now Faith" amid these challenges, not only as individuals but also as leaders, walking in the path God has set before us. It's important to recognize that having "Now Faith" doesn't always result in a change of direction; rather, it equips us to navigate the storms of life.

Understanding why God chose us for these storms helps us find purpose and meaning in our journey. Ultimately, we must learn to trust God rather than solely relying on our faith, as He is the source of our strength and guidance. With this understanding, we embrace faith as a powerful tool for our journey, allowing it to shape us into the individuals God intended us to be.

Learning to walk in "Now Faith" requires an unwavering commitment to God's principles and teachings. It is a continuous process of surrendering ourselves to His will and allowing Him to guide our steps. "Now Faith" empowers us to face the trials and tribulations that come our way, knowing that God is with us every step of the journey.

Furthermore, having "Now Faith" doesn't guarantee a smooth and effortless path. It means trusting God even when circumstances are challenging and uncertain. It's about relying on His strength and wisdom to overcome obstacles rather than solely on our understanding.

Moreover, understanding why God chose us for the storms helps us embrace the storms as opportunities for personal growth and spiritual development. It allows us to find meaning and purpose in our trials, knowing that God has a greater plan at work. Learning to always trust God, not just our faith, is crucial. Our faith is a valuable tool, but God holds the power to transform our lives and lead us through difficult times.

By trusting Him, we cultivate a deep and abiding relationship that sustains us in every circumstance. Understanding and embracing faith now transforms our perspective and empowers us to live a life that reflects God's love, grace, and power. It becomes a guiding principle that shapes our decisions, actions, and interactions with others, allowing us to live a life of purpose and fulfillment.

Acknowledgements

I want to take a moment to express my heartfelt gratitude to the individuals who have played significant roles in my life and supported me throughout the journey of writing this book.

First and foremost, my deepest gratitude goes to the God Almighty for his inspiration, wisdom, and discernment he has bestowed upon me throughout this writing journey. Your word has been a constant source of truth and guidance, illuminating the path before me and infusing these pages with divine wisdom.

I extend my deepest appreciation to my beloved wife, Suzanne, whose unwavering love, encouragement, and understanding have been a constant source of strength and inspiration. Your presence in my life is a blessing, and I am grateful for your unwavering support.

I want to honor the memory of my late father, Henry R. Turner Jr. Though he is no longer with us, his wisdom, guidance, and love resonate within me. His legacy of faith and resilience has shaped the person I am today, and I am forever grateful for his profound impact on my life.

To my mother, Mildred Turner, who is still with us, thank you for your unconditional love, prayers, and unwavering belief in me. Your constant support and encouragement have been a guiding light throughout this writing process. Your faith and strength inspire me daily.

I am grateful for my church family at TGPWC (The Gathering Place Worship Center). Your love, fellowship, and spiritual guidance have nurtured my faith and provided a community where I can grow and thrive. Thank you for embracing me as a family member and a source of encouragement and inspiration.

To all my dear friends and family, thank you for your love, encouragement, and belief in me. Your words of encouragement, prayers, and presence in my life have been invaluable. I am blessed to have you by my side, and your unwavering support has sustained me through the highs and lows of this writing journey.

I would also like to acknowledge my children and grandchildren, whose love and understanding have brought me immeasurable joy. Your presence and the beautiful moments we share have inspired me to pursue my dreams and make a positive difference in the world. You are the greatest blessing in my life, and I am honored to be your parent and grandparent.

Finally, I would like to appreciate my dear friend, Frank J. Williams, deeply. Your unwavering belief in me, words of wisdom, and constant encouragement have been invaluable. Your friendship has been a source of inspiration and strength, and I am grateful to have you in my life.

To all those who have touched my life, whether mentioned here or not, thank you for your love, support, and presence. Your belief in me and willingness to walk alongside me on this journey have meant the world to me. I am humbled and grateful for every one of you.

May God bless you abundantly for the love, support, and encouragement you have shown me throughout this endeavor.

With heartfelt gratitude,

Dr. Jevon Turner Sr.

About the Author

I am Dr. Jevon Turner, faithfully serving the vibrant congregation of The Gathering Place Worship Center in the beautiful city of Athens, Alabama. From the tender age of twelve, I felt an undeniable calling to proclaim the gospel and share the boundless love of God with all who would listen. Now, after thirty-nine years in the ministry, I firmly believe that God's word can transform lives and bring hope to the darkest corners of our world.

My journey in faith has been one of continuous learning and growth. Driven by an insatiable thirst for spiritual knowledge, I pursued and obtained a PhD in Theology, a testament to the grace of God working within me. This academic achievement has equipped me with a deep understanding of God's word, enabling me to guide my congregation with wisdom and discernment.

My unwavering conviction lies in the fact that the love of God knows no boundaries. We are called to share His love, compassion, and grace with everyone. I have witnessed firsthand the transformative power of God's word as broken hearts find healing, lives find purpose, and the lost find their way back to the loving embrace of their Creator.

When I stand before the congregation, I strive to deliver sermons that engage both the mind and the heart. Drawing from biblical wisdom, personal experiences, and practical application, I aim to captivate the audience and leave them inspired to pursue a life rooted in faith and guided by God's eternal truth. Through my words, I hope to ignite a spark in the hearts of those who listen, sparking a desire to walk alongside me on this incredible journey of faith.

As the visionary leader of The Gathering Place Worship Center, I have fostered a community where individuals from all walks of life can come together as a family united in our shared belief in Jesus Christ. Our church is not just a building but a sanctuary of love, acceptance, and spiritual empowerment. Within these walls, we find solace in His presence, grow in our relationship with Him, and become beacons of His light in our community.

Beyond the pulpit, I engage in counseling sessions, outreach initiatives, and personal connections to minister to the needs of those around me. My mission is to embody and exemplify the love of God in all aspects of my life, reaching out to the hurting, the lost, and the marginalized, offering them hope and a renewed sense of purpose.

I invite you to join me on this incredible journey of faith as we discover together the joy, peace, and fulfillment that can only be found in a life fully devoted to God. Let us embrace the transformative power of His love, allowing it to shape our lives and empower us to make a lasting impact in our communities. Together, let us shine brightly as reflections of His grace, spreading the love of God far and wide and forever changing lives for His glory.